LET'S DO LITERACY
WHAT IS FAMILIAR
YEAR 1 UNIT 1
AGES 4/6

Denise Pearse

ISBN: 9781697913026

DEDICATION

To all my wonderful family and friends.
You have given me so much support and encouragement along the way. Thank you for putting up with me during the writing of this book. And the previous books.

CONTENTS

1 INTRODUCTION

This is the first of six units in the Year 1 collection.

A six week plus literacy unit that that has a theme of 'What is Familiar'.
The national curriculum areas covered for each activity will be shown to help see progression.

The plans have been set to cover a five-day week, but that does not mean that you must work for five days without a break. The days are not listed Monday to Friday but are numbered 1 to 5.

Next to each activity is a box that you can use to record the date or a smiley face if all went well. Some activities might need to be revisited – or some work suggested for a day might need to be covered over two or more days. Take it at your child's pace.

Writing: For the writing task, work with your child. A lot of children find writing very difficult and need encouragement and support. Share the writing as much as you need to. Encourage good handwriting as much as is possible. Help with the understanding of how to set text out, and how to write for different purposes. But try to make the writing as fun as possible and avoid too much stress. Yes, being able to write is important – but understanding is more important.
The book I would recommend for handwriting practice at this stage is 'Handwriting Practice Book by Schofield and Sims'. Try to practice a little handwriting each day.

Make use of the technology you have available to you. A lot of the work can be done using a word processor or a presentation program like Power Point. Use cameras to record work and to make video clips. Search You Tube for the video versions of the books you read together.

Discussion is a very important element of literacy and these will be developed as they discuss their reading with you as well as their writing. It might also be useful to discuss with them what they will be learning at each stage and encourage them to talk about their learning.

Preparation: Gather as many books both fiction, poetry and non-fiction as you can. A visit to the library is always exciting. I have put in a suggested book list that you might consider, and I have left space for you to add your own.

Reading: Try to read a little each day. If you get chance, try to read the text first yourself so you know what questions to ask. I find it useful to use post-it notes when thinking of questions relating to the text to stick in the back of the book until I'm ready to use them.
The activity sheets at the back of the book can be used as guidelines or they can be photocopied. If you want coloured versions of all the activity sheets used here in PDF format, then pop along to www.whyplay.co and click on the tab – extra for books.

Year 1 (ages 4 to 6)

In this six-week block of work the areas covered will be;

Stories with predictable phrasing

Labels, list and captions

Recounts

Poetry – free verse

Suggested Reading List

We're Going on a Bear Hunt – Michael Rosen

Peace at Last – Jull Murphy

The Bad Tempered Ladybird – Eric Carle

The Gruffalo – Julia Donaldson and Axel Scheffler

Hairy Maclary – Lynley Dodd

Oliver's Vegetables – Alison Bartlett and Vivian French

The Three Little Pigs

Red Riding Hood

Goldilocks and the Three Bears

Chicken Lickin

The Little Red Hen

The Giant Turnip

Sign up for Oxford Owl – some great free e-books for all ages.
https://www.oxfordowl.co.uk/

UK National Curriculum

These are taken from the National Curriculum for England. I know homeschoolers are under no obligation to follow the curriculum — but they do give a good grounding for our children's learning so can be used as guidelines of progression.

Reading – Word Reading
Apply phonic knowledge to decode words
respond speedily with the correct sound to graphemes (letters or groups of letters)
read words containing taught GPCs and –s, –es, –ing, –ed, –er and –est endings
read other words of more than one syllable
read words with contractions [for example, I'm, I'll, we'll], and understand that the apostrophe represents the omitted letter(s)

Reading - Comprehension
listening to and discussing a wide range of poems, stories and non-fiction at a level beyond that at which they can read independently
being encouraged to link what they read or hear read to their own experiences
becoming very familiar with key stories, fairy stories and traditional tales, retelling them and considering their particular characteristics
recognising and joining in with predictable phrases
learning to appreciate rhymes and poems, and to recite some by heart
discussing word meanings, linking new meanings to those already known
checking that the text makes sense to them as they read
discussing the significance of the title and events
predicting what might happen on the basis of what has been read so far
participate in discussion about what is read to them, taking turns and listening to what others say
explain clearly their understanding of what is read to them.

Writing – Transcription Spelling

segmenting spoken words into phonemes and representing these by graphemes, spelling many correctly

learning new ways of spelling phonemes for which one or more spellings are already known, and learn some words with each spelling, including a few common homophones

learning to spell common exception words

learning to spell more words with contracted forms

learning the possessive apostrophe (singular) [for example, the girl's book]

distinguishing between homophones and near homophones

add suffixes to spell longer words, including –ment, –ness, –ful, –less, –ly

write from memory simple sentences dictated that include common exception words and punctuation taught so far.

Handwriting

form lower-case letters of the correct size relative to one another

start using some of the diagonal and horizontal strokes needed to join letters and understand which letters, when adjacent to one another, are best left unjoined

write capital letters and digits of the correct size, orientation and relationship to one another and to lower case letters

use spacing between words that reflects the size of the letters.

Writing - Composition

writing narratives about personal experiences and those of others (real and fictional)

writing about real events

writing poetry

writing for different purposes

planning or saying out loud what they are going to write about

writing down ideas and/or key words, including new vocabulary

encapsulating what they want to say, sentence by sentence

proof-reading to check for errors in spelling, grammar and punctuation [for example, ends of sentences punctuated correctly]

read aloud what they have written with appropriate intonation to make the meaning clear.

Writing – Vocabulary, Grammar and Punctuation

learning how to use both familiar and new punctuation correctly, including full stops, capital letters, exclamation marks, question marks, commas for lists and apostrophes for contracted forms and the possessive (singular)

sentences with different forms: statement, question, exclamation, command

expanded noun phrases to describe and specify [for example, the blue butterfly]

the present and past tenses correctly and consistently including the progressive form

subordination (using when, if, that, or because) and co-ordination (using or, and, or but)

Detail of content to be introduced

Word	Regular plural noun suffixes –s or –es [for example, dog, dogs; wish, wishes], including the effects of these suffixes on the meaning of the noun Suffixes that can be added to verbs where no change is needed in the spelling of root words (e.g. helping, helped, helper) How the prefix un– changes the meaning of verbs and adjectives [negation, for example, unkind, or undoing: untie the boat]
Sentence	How words can combine to make sentences Joining words and joining clauses using 'and'
Text	Sequencing sentences to form short narratives
Punctuation	Separation of words with spaces Introduction to capital letters, full stops, question marks and exclamation marks to demarcate sentences Capital letters for names and for the personal pronoun I
Terminology	letter, capital letter word, singular, plural sentence punctuation, full stop, question mark, exclamation mark

Remember these should only be used as guidelines. All children learn at different rates.

Here are some 'I Can' Statements to help you check for understanding.

Tick Box	I can listen to a story and respond with memories
	I can compare stories
	I can talk about settings
	I can tell a story based on a personal experience
	I can talk about writing
	I can write a story with more than one sentence
	I can re-enact a story
	I can compare stories and say what is my favourite
	I can retell a story
	I can answer questions about a text
	I can write a recount in order
	I know that a sentence has a capital letter to start
	I can leave spaces between my words
	I can use a full stop at the end of my sentence
	I can recite rhymes with repeating patterns
	I can write an acrostic poem
	I can identify rhyming words
	I can tell you what a noun is
	I can tell you what a verb is
	I can tell you what an adjective is
	I can use phonics to sound out words when reading
	I can spell some new words by sounding out
	I can select books for reading
	I can use a word program to type up my work with help

Day 1

Introduction:

Explain that you will be looking at a book together.

Introduce the book and have a good look at the front cover. Talk about the title – the authors name and the illustrators name. You could use one of the suggested books like 'The Three Little Pigs' or 'We're going on a Bear Hunt' for this, or any other book that has some repeating language.

Explain that you will be thinking about who the characters are in the story and the setting. (you might need to explain what characters and settings are).

Main Task:

Discuss and model good reading techniques, pointing to the words, using pictures and sounding words out to decode.
Read the book together. Encourage them to read any words they are familiar with and help them to sound out any that are more difficult.
When you have finished reading together discuss the book. How did we learn about the character? How else does the author tell the reader about characters? (Draw out the author uses words to create pictures in our heads and sometimes pictures are used as well to help us understand the story)
Model using their ideas to write a sentence.

Independent Work:

Ask them to draw their favourite character from the book. Now encourage them to write a sentence about the character underneath.
To make it easier, share the writing. Make it a game and write one word each.
(Remind them about spaces in between words and capital letters to begin sentences)

Plenary:

Talk about their drawing and why they chose that character.
Ask about the setting and recap on what happened in the story.
Look for the story on You Tube and watch it together.

Familiar Stories

- ❑ Apply phonic knowledge to decode words.
- ❑ listening to and discuss a wide range of stories
- ❑ recognising and joining in with predictable phrases
- ❑ checking that the text makes sense to them as they read
- ❑ form lower-case letters of the correct size relative to one another
- ❑ use spacing between words that reflects the size of the letters.
- ❑ planning or saying out loud what they are going to write about

Spelling rules for this week's words.

The sounds /f/, /l/, /s/, /z/ and /k/ spelt ff, ll, ss, zz and ck

The /f/, /l/, /s/, /z/ and /k/ sounds are usually spelt as ff, ll, ss, zz and ck if they come straight after a single vowel letter in short words. Exceptions: if, pal, us, bus, yes.

Spelling

Read these words together.   **off - puff - huff - cuff – cliff – sniff - stuff**

Try to think of a silly sentence to go with each of the words.
You write the sentences out leaving a gap where the spelling word goes. Ask them to write the spelling in the gap using bright colours.

WEEK 1

Day 2

Introduction:
Talk about the story you read together yesterday.
Q. Can you remember the characters?
Q. Can you remember where the story took place?

Explain that you will be reading another book together today, and this time you are really going to think about the setting.

Familiar Stories

- ❑ Apply phonic knowledge to decode words.
- ❑ listening to and discuss a wide range of stories
- ❑ recognising and joining in with predictable phrases
- ❑ checking that the text makes sense to them as they read
- ❑ form lower-case letters of the correct size relative to one another
- ❑ planning or saying out loud what they are going to write about
- ❑ writing down ideas and/or key words, including new vocabulary

Main Task:
Read the new book together. Encourage them to read any words they are familiar with and help them to sound out any that are more difficult.
When you have finished reading together discuss the book.
Q. Where did this story happen? (setting)
Q. Can we think about some really good words to describe the setting? **(adjectives).** Write the adjectives down as they say them.
You will find some suggested adjectives on Activity Sheet 1

Independent Work:
Ask them to draw the settings from the story in the order of the story.
To make it easier they could just draw the main setting from the book.

Label the drawing with **adjectives** that will help describe it.

Plenary:
Recap on what happened in the story. Use the book to remind them the sequence of events.
Q. Do you think you chose good adjectives to describe the setting?
Look for the story on You Tube and watch it together.

Handwriting:
Practise handwriting using the spelling words for this week.
off - puff - huff - cuff – cliff – sniff - stuff

Spelling
Practise some of this week's spelling words on **Activity Sheet 2**. -off-cliff-huff-puff
(The words can be cut out and stuck into the correct places)

EXTRA: Read together or watch a You Tube version of The Three Little Pigs. Ask them to shout out when they hear a 'ff' sound.

- ❑ recognising and joining in with predictable phrases

You will need to get together some photos of trips out for the main activity today.

Year 1 Unit 1

WEEK1

Day 3

Warm Up:

Write a question mark, an exclamation mark and a full stop of small pieces of card. Talk about what these symbols mean.

Make up sentences and ask them to hold up **? ! or .**

To show what kind of sentences it is.
For example: It is raining outside   Is it raining   It's raining

Introduction:

Talk about a day out. Look at the photos together.
Introduce the word RECOUNT. Explain that a recount is about events that happened in the past– like their trip out.
Read together **Activity Sheet 3** Features of a Recount

Main Task:

Discuss drawing pictures of their day out in order (or use photos from the day). Point out the words at the top of each box on **Activity Sheet 4**. Talk about them being **'time connectives'** because they tell us what time something happened.

Independent Work:

With help from you ask them to draw the events of the day in order.
Encourage them to write a short sentence or word at the bottom of each picture that tells the reader what is happening. (If writing is difficult then you scribe the sentence for them)

Plenary:

Look at their recount together. Does it show what happened in the day?

EXTRA:

Read together a book of their choice.
While reading look for any question marks or exclamation marks.

Handwriting:

Practise a little handwriting each day, but try to make it fun

Punctuation

- ☐ sentences with different forms: statement, question, exclamation,

Recount

- ☐ writing narratives about personal experiences and those of others (real and fictional)
- ☐ writing about real events
- ☐ planning or saying out loud what they are going to write about
- ☐ Separation of words with spaces Introduction to capital letters, full stops, question marks and exclamation marks to demarcate sentences Capital letters for names and for the personal pronoun I

Reading

- ☐ recognising and joining in with predictable phrases
- ☐ listening to and discussing a wide range of poems, stories and non-fiction at a level beyond that at which they can read independently

Day 4

Warm Up:
Talk about your favourite books.
Can you name some of the characters in the books?
Which characters do you like the best?
Talk about why you like them the best.

Introduction:
Remind them of the recount they wrote during the last lesson.
They wrote a personal recount of a trip out.
Another kind of personal recount is a diary. Look again at
Activity Sheet 3 to remind them of what to think about when
writing a recount.
Explain that today they are going to be writing a recount of what
happened yesterday starting with getting out of bed.
Section off four squares in their book or use **Activity Sheet 4**

Main Task:
Ask them to think about getting out of bed in the morning and
draw their first picture of that.
Encourage them to write a short sentence or word to describe the
picture. Practice sleepy faces at each other.
Discuss other events of the day and the order in which they
happened then ask them to fill out the rest of the boxes.

Plenary:
Look at their recount together. Does it show what happened in
the day?

Spelling
Have a look again at this week's spellings.
Explain that you will be doing a test tomorrow to see if they can
remember how to spell them.
Use felt tips or paints to write out the words in bubble writing on
a large piece of paper. Talk about any patterns then can see in
the words.
Draw together an image to go with each word.
Encourage sounding out of letters.

EXTRA:
Read together a book of their choice.
Share the reading – reading one page each.
Model intonation when reading.

Recount

- ❑ writing narratives about personal experiences and those of others (real and fictional)
- ❑ writing about real events
- ❑ planning or saying out loud what they are going to write about
- ❑ Separation of words with spaces Introduction to capital letters, full stops, question marks and exclamation marks to demarcate sentences Capital letters for names and for the personal pronoun I

Spelling

- ❑ segmenting spoken words into phonemes and representing

Reading
- ❑ recognising and joining in with predictable phrases
- ❑ listening to and discussing a wide range of poems, stories and non-fiction at a level beyond that at which they can read independently

Handwriting:

10

WEEK 1

Day 5

Introduction:
Discuss Capital letters and full stops.
Where do we use capital letters? Where do we use full stops?

Main Task:
Fill out Activity Sheet 5 and put back the capital letters and full stops where they are missing.

Plenary:
Have a talk about how different capital letters are to small letters.
Write down the alphabet in capitals and ask them to copy the letters underneath.

Capital Letters and Full Stops
- ❏ Separation of words with spaces Introduction to capital letters, full stops, question marks and exclamation marks to demarcate sentences Capital letters for names and for the personal pronoun I
- ❏ form lower-case letters of the correct size relative to one another
- ❏ use spacing between words that reflects the size of the letters

Spelling
Testing of the spelling words for this week.

off - puff - huff - cuff – cliff – sniff - stuff
There are many ways to can do the spelling test depending on how well you think they are going to do with the words. Get them to sound out the phonemes as they write. If they want to write out the spelling in felt tips on pieces of card – then why not. If they want to type the words out – then that's OK. If they want to write them as a list – then that's good too. It is the remembering of the spellings that's important, not how they write them down.

Handwriting:
Make handwriting practise fun today. Draw some swirly lines for them to copy over.

EXTRA:
Read together a book of their choice.

Notes and Assessment of week

Day 1

Warm Up:
Shout out all the characters that live in your house or are part of the family.
Explain that they are characters in real life and that characters in books can be from real life or they can be made up.

Introduction: Familiar Characters and Settings
For this task use a book called 'Oliver's Vegetables' by Alison Bartlett and Vivian French. Take a visit to the library or you will be able to find the story on You Tube if you don't want to get the book.
Of course, you can use any book you want but follow the same ideas.
        As you are reading talk about the characters in the book.

Main Task:
Ask them to draw a picture of their chosen character and write a sentence about him/her. Remind them to sound out words.
Extend this by asking them to write 3-5 sentences about their chosen character. Remind them to use the pronoun he or she instead of the name. Encourage imaginative vocabulary.
To make this task easier, use a word processing program and help them type up the sentences. (The sentences can be printed out and pasted at the bottom of the pictures).

Plenary:
Talk about the character they have chosen. Discuss how the character was feeling during the story. Look back at the story to reinforce their ideas.

Characters
- ❑ Apply phonic knowledge to Apply phonic knowledge to decode words
- ❑ being encouraged to link what they read or hear read to their own experiences
- ❑ How words can combine to make sentences Joining words and joining clauses using 'and'
- ❑ Separation of words with spaces Introduction to capital letters, full stops, question marks and exclamation marks to demarcate sentences Capital letters for names and for the personal pronoun I

Spelling
Read these words together.   **miss - hiss - less - if - us - bus – yes**

Try to think of a silly sentence to go with each of the words.
You write the sentences out leaving a gap where the spelling word goes. Ask them to write the spelling in the gap using bright colours.

Spelling rules for this week's words.
The sounds /f/, /l/, /s/, /z/ and /k/ spelt ff, ll, ss, zz and ck
The /f/, /l/, /s/, /z/ and /k/ sounds are usually spelt as ff, ll, ss, zz and ck if they come straight after a single vowel letter in short words.
Exceptions: if, pal, us, bus, yes.

EXTRA: Read together a book of their choice.

While reading take special notice of the characters.

Day 2

Warm Up:

Talk about yesterday's story. It was all about vegetables. Can they tell you the vegetables they like or don't like?

Using **Activity Sheet 6** – Ask them to draw the vegetables they remember from the story 'Oliver's Vegetables'. (they do not have to be in order because they are going to be cut out)

Introduction:

Talk about the story of 'Oliver's Vegetables'. Discuss the order of the events. Read through the book again to remind them of the order of events.

Help them to cut out their pictures of the vegetables.

Main Task:

Paste the pictures of the vegetables in order in the prepared sheets. **Activity sheets 7 to 13**. Ask them to draw the characters and to write a sentence for each day of the week.

Extend this by asking them to think of an adjective to describe the vegetables. E.g. juicy carrots.

What other adjectives can you think of?

To make it easier, share the writing task if needed.

Remind them to leave spaces in between words and to use a full stop at the end of the sentence.

Extra:

Computer practice.

Together, type of the days of the week on a word processing program.

Demonstrate how to change font size, change colour and how to make sure the word has a capital letter at the beginning.

Demonstrate how to print out their days of the week for a display.

Recall of Text

❑ being encouraged to being encouraged to link what they read or hear read to their own experiences

Sequencing

❑ being encouraged to link being encouraged to link what they read or hear read to their own experiences

❑ discussing word meanings, linking new meanings to those already known

❑ segmenting spoken words into phonemes and representing these by graphemes, spelling many correctly

❑ write capital letters and digits of the correct size, orientation and relationship to one another and to lower case letters

❑ planning or saying out loud what they are going to write about

❑ read aloud what they have written with appropriate intonation to make the meaning clear.

Handwriting:

Practise a little handwriting each day, but try to make it fun

WEEK 2

Warm Up:
Think of some rhyming words together to go with the words **miss, hiss and less**

Write these words at the top of a large sheet of paper – make them bright and colourful.
When they say a word that rhymes, ask them to write that word down. To make it easier write the word down for them.
Encourage them to write a word in big colourful letters.

Introduction:
Talk about the books you read together over the last two weeks and the story of 'Oliver's Vegetables'.
Have a look at the covers and some of the pages to help them recall what the stories were about. Ask them to choose the book they liked the best. Talk about the characters in the chosen book.
Q. Why do you like that character?
Q. Where did the story take place?

Main Task:
Talk about what a book review is. Tell them you are going to be writing a book review together.
See Activity Sheet 14.
Encourage them to complete the sentences and to draw the front cover of the book.

Extra:
Make puppets of their chosen story and act it out together.
Or
Video them reading out pages from their chosen book.
Encourage

Read together a book of their choice.

While reading take special notice of the punctuation used.

Handwriting:
Go over any letters they are having problems with

Spelling
segmenting spoken words into phonemes and representing these by graphemes.

Book Review
- ❑ becoming very familiar with key stories, fairy stories and traditional tales, retelling them and considering their particular characteristics
- ❑ discussing the significance of the title and events
- ❑ form lower-case letters of the correct size relative to one another
- ❑ use spacing between words that reflects the size of the letters.
- ❑ writing for different purposes
- ❑ planning or saying out loud what they are going to write about

Reading or Telling the story
- ❑ read aloud what they have written with appropriate intonation to make the meaning clear.
- ❑ Apply phonic knowledge to decode words
- ❑ respond speedily with the correct sound to graphemes (letters or groups of letters)
- ❑ discussing word meanings, linking new meanings to those already known

Day 4

Warm Up:
Once again play the game with the question mark, exclamation mark and full stop cards.
Write a question mark, an exclamation mark and a full stop of small pieces of card. Talk about what these symbols mean.

Make up sentences and ask them to hold up **? ! or .** To show what kind of sentences it is.
For example: It is raining outside   Is it raining   It's raining
Ask them to think of sentences to ask you.
Talk about these sentences being – A statement – A command – A question.

Introduction:
Talk about what foods an alien or a pirate would like to eat.
Write their ideas down. Encourage them to think of some really funny foods.

Main Task:
Explain that you are going to write a story together. You will do some of the writing for them and they can do some writing as well. Explain that you really would like their ideas because it will be a much better story that way.
At the top of the page write the title depending on what character they choose. E.g**. I am a Pirate**
Now start each line with:
On Monday I ate…….
On Tuesday I ate ….
Etc.
Remind them that days of the week have a capital letter.
Encourage the use of adjectives to describe the food.

Example: On Monday I ate some juicy seagull pie
Explain that because it is a story, they can make up any kind of food they like, and it does not have to be real.
Introduce the term **fiction.**

EXTRA: When their story is finished, ask them to illustrate it.

Read together a book of their choice.
While reading take special notice of adjectives used.

Punctuation
- ❑ sentences with different forms: statement, question, exclamation, command

Story Writing
- ❑ segmenting spoken words into phonemes and representing these by graphemes, spelling many correctly
- ❑ form lower-case letters of the correct size relative to one another
- ❑ use spacing between words that reflects the size of the letters.
- ❑ writing for different purposes
- ❑ planning or saying out loud what they are going to write about
- ❑ encapsulating what they want to say, sentence by sentence
- ❑ expanded noun phrases to describe and specify [for example, the blue butterfly]
- ❑ How words can combine to make sentences Joining words and joining clauses using 'and'

Reading or Telling the story
- ❑ discussing word meanings, linking new meanings to those already known

15

WEEK 2

Day 5

Introduction: Grammar

Explain that a noun is a word that names things. Ask them to look around the room and point at objects and say what they are.

Play a game of 'I spy'

Main Task:

Go to Activity Sheet 15. Talk about the pictures and the nouns they can see.

Encourage them to write the noun under each picture.

Spelling

Testing of the spelling words for this week.

miss - hiss - less - if - us - bus – yes

There are many ways to can do the spelling test depending on how well you think they are going to do with the words. Get them to sound out the phonemes as they write. If they want to write out the spelling in felt tips on pieces of card – then why not.

Try using scrabble tiles or letters cut out on small card – or invest in some magnetic letters and use them for spellings.

- ❑ segmenting spoken words into phonemes and representing these by graphemes, spelling many correctly
- ❑ form lower-case letters of the correct size relative to one another
- ❑ writing for different purposes
- ❑ planning or saying out loud what they are going to write about
- ❑ understanding that nouns are names for objects.

Handwriting:

Make handwriting practise fun today. Paint capital letters using glue and then sprinkle glitter on top before it dries.

Notes and Assessment of week

CHAPTER 3 WEEK 3

Day 1

Warm Up:
Recap on nouns by playing 'I spy'. Remind them what nouns are. Ask them to see how many nouns they can touch or bring back to you in a minute.
Have a look around the room – Find 10 nouns.

❑ understanding that nouns are names for objects.

Introduction:
Read together a book of your choice. Something like 'The Three Little Pigs', or 'Little Red Hen'. It would be better if it is a story they are familiar with.

Main Task:
Ask how the characters felt in the story. Do they think they are happy, sad, excited, scared etc.?
Draw some circles on a page for them and ask them to draw faces showing different emotions. Their very own emojis.

Labels
❑ form lower-case letters of the correct size relative to one another
❑ writing for different purposes
❑ planning or saying out loud what they are going to write about
❑ encapsulating what they want to say,

Plenary:
Talk about how they
Are feeling today.

Ask them to label their emojis with the correct feeling words underneath.

Handwriting:
Today look at any capital letters they are having problems with.
Model how to write the letters.

Spelling
Read these words together. **well - pull - full - wall**
buzz - fizz - back - stick - flick – pal

Write out the words in bright colours on small pieces of card.
Turn the cards face down. Take turns to pick up a card and read it.
Demonstrate how to sound out the phonemes.

Spelling rules for this week's words.
The /f/, /l/, /s/, /z/ and /k/ sounds are usually spelt as ff, ll, ss, zz and ck if they come straight after a single vowel letter in short words.

EXTRA:
Try using a drawing package on the computer to design some emojis. Print them out and stick them in the book.

ICT skills
Using a paint program with pre-set shapes.
How to choose different colours.
How to use the print

Handwriting:
Make it fun

Day 2

Warm Up:
Reading CVC words. See **activity sheet 16** for the letter sounds covered in phase 3.
This is a recap of phonics from phase 3.
Work on sounding out phonics and writing words
Activity Sheet 17
Encourage sounding out of the words.

Phonics
❑ Apply phonic knowledge to decode words
❑ respond speedily with the correct sound to graphemes (letters or groups of letters)

Introduction:
Talk about feelings and the work from yesterday where they made their own emojis.
Talk about why we have certain feelings. Is it because something has happened? Is it because we are in a certain place? Is it because of someone else?

Main Task:
Take it in turns to act out how you might feel in certain situations. Use lots of facial expressions to show your emotion. It would be a good idea to use a mirror with this activity. As you are taking it in turns to show different emotions – you **write them down**. Explain that these adjectives can be used when you write to make your writing more interesting. **(scared, shocked, happy, tired, angry….)** Think of some scenarios where you might feel different emotions.
For example:
I saw a tiger and I was …
I had a big cake for my birthday, and I was …
I fell and grazed my knee and I was …
I ran all the way home and I was …
Her brother jumped out from behind the bush and she was …

Encourage them to think of some situations and get you to act out the emotion when it is their turn.

Role Play
❑ being encouraged to link what they read or hear read to their own experiences
❑ discussing word meanings, linking new meanings to those already known
❑ discussing and acting out a range of emotions
❑ Understanding more about describing words.

Extra – ICT
Ask them to type up the feeling adjectives using different colours and different fonts that they can glue into their books to look back on.

Plenary:
You would have created a word bank of adjectives that they will be able to use in their writing. Read them through together.

Read together a book of their choice.
Try to spot where the author lets us know how the character is feeling.

Spelling
Read the spelling words for this week and sound them out.

18

WEEK 3

Day 3

Warm Up:
Discuss characters they know from films and books.
(You could make a list or they could draw them)
Were they the main character in the story?
Explain that the main character in a story has a very fancy name.

The main character is called the **protagonist**
Tell them to ask family members when they see them if they know what a protagonist is.

Introduction:
Look at the word bank of feeling adjectives from last lesson. Ask them to pick any feeling they want,
Now ask them to think of a name for a character. It can be a character from a story or film they already know but, try and get them to think of their own character.

Main Task:
Demonstrate how they could start a story about this character.
For example:

One day, Molly was feeling happy.
Now talk about why she might be feeling this way.
She had a new puppy.
Next show them how they might finish their story.
She loved her puppy very much and always looked after him.

Encourage them to write the first line of their story (or write it together). Then the next line. And then the last.

Plenary:
Read through the story and talk about the character. Did you like the character? Did you show how she was feeling?

Reading comprehension
See **Activity Sheet 18**. Read through the text together. Now look at the questions. Ask them to find the words in the text that answer the questions and underline them.
Next, ask them to write the answers in the spaces.

Extra:
Choose a film to watch together.
While you are watching the film talk about the characters and the settings.
Ask them if they can tell you who the **protagonist** it.
Remind them that the protagonist is the main character.

Characters
- ❑ participate in discussion about what is read to them
- ❑ understanding the term character

Adjectives
- ❑ being encouraged to link what they read or hear read to their own experiences
- ❑ learning how to use both familiar and new punctuation correctly , including full stops, capital letters, exclamation marks, question marks
- ❑ Sequencing sentences to form short narratives
- ❑ Separation of words with spaces Introduction to capital letters, full stops, question marks and exclamation marks to demarcate sentences Capital letters for names and for the personal pronoun I

Reading
- ❑ Apply phonic knowledge to decode words
- ❑ respond speedily with the correct sound to graphemes (letters or groups of letters)
- ❑ explain clearly their understanding of what is read to them.

WEEK 3

Day 4

Warm Up:

Look at the reading comprehension **Activity Sheet 18** again.

Talk about what might happen next in the story.

Take it in turns to each say the next part of the story. Follow their lead and carry on the story from where they left off.

For Example, the story could go something like this.

You – Bobby and his sister looked out of the window. They wanted to be the first one to see the sea.

At last, they reached the seaside. They all scrambled out of the car. Dad grabbed the picnic basket and mum grabbed the picnic blanket. They all went down to the sand.

Them – They sat down to eat their lunch.

You – Just then, a large crab started side stepping towards them. He wanted their lunch. Dad, who was very brave, rushed over to pick the crab up.

Them – The crab pinched dad on the finger……..

Make the story as fantastical as you like. Encourage them to think of new and wonderful things that could happen.

Telling a story orally is very important. It develops their listening skills and helps them to build on a story structure. It can also be a lot of fun.

Story Telling
- ❑ participate in discussion about what is read to them
- ❑ predicting what might happen on the basis of what has been read so far
- ❑ explain clearly their understanding of what is read to them.
- ❑ Join in a story orally

Story Telling
- ❑ writing for different purposes
- ❑ planning or saying out loud what they are going to write about
- ❑ writing down ideas and/or key words, including new vocabulary

Main Task:

Ask them to draw part of their story, including the characters. They can then label different parts of the picture or write a sentence underneath.

Plenary:

Ask questions about the story you invented together.

Q. Was Bobby still happy in our story?

Q. What would have happened if …?

Q. How could we have made the story more exciting?

Handwriting:

Practice letters they are having problems with

Extra:

Split a sheet of paper in four. You can later stick this sheet into the front of their writing book. Ask them to think about words they can use for – settings, characters, feelings and objects in stories that they might like to use. You can write these words out as a reference for later use when they start making up longer stories for themselves.

For example:

Settings – dark cave, sandy beach, creepy woods …

Characters – prince, princess, boy, giant, gnome …

Feelings – scared, happy, excited, shocked …

Objects – crown, magic lamp, beanstalk,

WEEK 3

Day 5

Introduction: Grammar
Recap on what a noun is.
Explain that the days of the week are proper nouns, so they always start with a capital letter.
Ask them if they think the months of the year are proper nouns.

Main Task:
Look at a calendar that shows a month on the page if you have one (you can easily find one online if you do not have one you can use).
Look at how the page is set out. Point out that sometimes the days of the week use shortened words. (Mon, Tues, Wed, Thur, Fri, Sat and Sun).
Paint, crayon or felt tip the days of the week as a poster. Encourage them to be as creative as they like. They can use the shortened way of writing the days, or the full version – but they must remember to use a capital letter at the beginning.

Spelling
Testing of spelling words for this week.

well - pull - full - wall - buzz - fizz - back - stick - flick – pal

Encourage them the sound out the words before they write them. If they find writing difficult then encourage them to type the words of use plastic letters.

Grammar
- ❑ Beginning to understand some of the grammar terms used
- ❑ Understanding that names need a capital letter, including days and months
- ❑ Becoming more confident with writing words
- ❑ Understanding that some words can be shortened
- ❑ learning how to use both familiar and new punctuation correctly , including full stops, capital letters, exclamation marks, question marks

Notes and Assessment of week

CHAPTER 4 WEEK 4

Day 1

Warm Up:
Talk about what verbs are and that they are needed in every sentence.
There are three types of verb (action, linking and helping), but for now they only need to focus on the action verb.

Point to different parts of your bodies. Using a verb say what that part does.
The eyes see. The foot kicks. The belly wobbles.
Now think of some actions you can do.
I can run. I can sing. I can laugh. I can hop.
Take it in turns to write down the verbs as you say them.

Introduction:
Read 'Chicken Licken' – Talk about the repeated pattern (The sky is falling, and we are going to tell the king)
Encourage them to say this line with you every time you read it in the story.
Q. Do these repeating sentences make the story more fun?
Q. Do these repeating sentences make the story easier to remember?
Q. How do you think the characters feel in the story?
Q. What do you think about the main character (protagonist)

Main Task:
Ask them to draw the characters in the story and them cut them out. If they need help with the cutting part, then do it for them. They are now going to stick them in their book in the correct order the appear in the story. Starting of course with Chicken Licken.
Ask them to write the name of each animal underneath the picture. Encourage them to sound out the spellings of the words or show them the words in the story so they can copy them.
Retell the story pointing to each character.

Plenary:
Watch the YouTube version of 'Chicken Licken'
Q. Is it the same as the story?
Q. What is different?

Spelling
Jumping - jumped – jump – buzz - buzzing – buzzed - look – looked - looking

VERBS
Main verbs or action verbs are used to express action; something that an animal, a person or a thing does. In each of the following sentences, we only have a main verb.

The moon <u>glows.</u>
The teddy <u>wriggles.</u>
The boy <u>jumps.</u>

Story
- [ ] listening to and discussing a wide range of poems, stories and non-fiction at a level beyond that at which they can read independently
- [ ] becoming very familiar with key stories, fairy stories and traditional tales, retelling them and considering their particular characteristics
- [ ] discussing word meanings, linking new meanings to those already known

Spelling rules for this week's words.
Adding the endings –ing, –ed and –er to verbs where no change is needed to the root word

Day 2

Warm Up:
Write out some verb cards. On each one put something you can do.

Suggested cards – **dance – sing – hop – read – wink – jump – sit – twirl – swim - jog**

Next write out some feeling cards

Suggested cards – **happily, crossly, sadly, shyly, angrily, silly, upset, worried**

Place the cards face down on the table. Take it in turns to pick one card from each pile. (If they have problems reading what's on the cards them help them out).
You now must act out the verb according to what's on the feelings card.
If you have more than two people playing this game, or if they manage to read the card without your help then – change it into **'Guess what the feeling is?'**

Verbs
- ❑ Beginning to understand verbs and how they are used in a sentence.
- ❑ Beginning to understand orally how verbs change depending on whether it is 'past', 'present' or 'future'

Introduction:
Read 'Gingerbread Man' together. **Activity Sheet 20 to 23.**
Encourage them to read the repeated text and any words they are becoming familiar with.

Main Task:
Cut out the characters from the story – **Activity Sheet 24** or encourage them to draw their own.
Encourage them to tell the story in their own words using the pictures, (If they need help remembering the sequence, then write it down for them).
Try filming them as they are acting out the story and use the video for discussion later.

Plenary:
Cut out the words, **Activity Sheet 19**, and use them to make a sentence.

Story
- ❑ Apply phonic knowledge to decode words
- ❑ read other words of more than one syllable
- ❑ listening to and discussing a wide range of poems, stories and non-fiction at a level beyond that at which they can read independently
- ❑ becoming very familiar with key stories, fairy stories and traditional tales, retelling them and considering their particular characteristics
- ❑ recognising and joining in with predictable phrases

Extra: ICT
Demonstrate how to open up a word processing program like WORD on the computer.
Ask them to type out the word for each of the characters in the story.
Encourage them to change font size and colour.
Print these out for the next lesson where they will be sequencing the story.

WEEK 4

Day 3

Warm Up:
Remind them of what the word 'verb' means.
Have a look at the verb cards you have already made. Talk about any more verbs you can add to your verb cards.
Talk about the stories you have read this week. Help them to think of some verbs that were in the story.
Chicken Liken **crying**, the little old lady **cooking**, the gingerbread man **running**, etc.
If you did make a video of them re-telling the Gingerbread Man story, watch it together and discuss it.

Introduction:
Read 'Gingerbread Man' to them. **Activity Sheet 20 to 23**.
Encourage them to join in with the repeated text.

Main Task:
Use the cut of images of the story characters and the character names they typed out.
Ask them to arrange them in order.
Stick them in order in their book.
EXTRA: encourage them to write a sentence for each image.

Plenary:
Discuss the settings in the story. Did the settings change?

Extra: ICT - research
Talk about making their own gingerbread men tomorrow.
Together look on the internet (or in recipe books) for recipes for gingerbread men.
There is a recipe on **activity sheet 25** for you to look at.
Talk about what you might need to buy to make gingerbread men.
Together write a shopping list.
(If you don't want to make gingerbread men – then talk about making the story characters out of playdough).

Read together a book of their choice.
Try to spot where the author lets us know how the character is feeling. Help to sound out words that are unfamiliar.

Verbs
- ❑ Beginning to understand verbs and how they are used in a sentence.
- ❑ Beginning to understand orally how verbs change depending on whether it is 'past', 'present' or 'future'

Story
- ❑ Apply phonic knowledge to decode words
- ❑ read other words of more than one syllable
- ❑ listening to and discussing a wide range of poems, stories and non-fiction at a level beyond that at which they can read independently
- ❑ becoming very familiar with key stories, fairy stories and traditional tales, retelling them and considering their particular characteristics
- ❑ recognising and joining in with predictable phrases

Handwriting:
Practice letters they are having problems with.
The book I would recommend for handwriting practice at this stage is 'Handwriting Practice Book by Schofield and Sims'.

Day 4

Warm Up:
Talk about whether cooking is a verb.
Discuss what other verbs you can think of to do with cooking.
Some of the words you might discuss are: beat, mix, melt, pour, blend.

Verbs
- [ ] Beginning to understand verbs and how they are used in a sentence.
- [ ] Beginning to understand orally how verbs change depending on whether it is 'past', 'present' or 'future'

Introduction:
Read through the recipe for a gingerbread man together.
Gather all the ingredients that are needed and put them on the table.
Encourage them to read the packets.

Main Task:
Help with measuring out all the ingredients needed and put them into bowls ready to use.
Follow the instructions together.
With help, let them mix all the ingredients together.
Roll out the dough and shape into gingerbread men.
While them are cooking take some photos for them to sequence in their books after the biscuits have been made.

Encourage them to decorate the biscuits in whatever way they want.

Plenary:
Discuss why the instructions were important.
Q. did the instructions have to be in a certain order?
Q. what could happen if we didn't follow the correct order?
Etc.

Instructions
- [ ] Beginning to understand instruction text
- [ ] listening to and discussing a wide range of poems, stories and non-fiction at a level beyond that at which they can read independently

Follow Up:
Help them write a title at the top of the page. **Gingerbread Man Recipe.**
Help them draw a picture of their cooked (or playdough) Gingerbread man.
Sequence the other photos taken while they were making their biscuits. (If you were unable to take photos, encourage them to draw the ingredients and bowls used)

Plenary:
Have a look together at their sequencing of the recipe.
Q. Did you leave anything out?
Q. How could you make the instructions clearer?
Q. Did you like the story?
Q. What other animals could he have met on the way?

Sequencing
- [ ] Beginning to understand instruction text
- [ ] becoming very familiar with key stories, fairy stories and traditional tales, retelling them and considering their particular characteristics
- [ ] Extending the text

Day 5

Introduction: Grammar
Recap on what a verb is.

Main Task:
Talk about the verb game you played during the week.
Ask them if they can remember any verbs. (doing words).
Act out some verbs together.

Spelling
Testing of the spelling words for this week.

Jumping – jumped – jump – buzz – buzzing – buzzed – look – looked - looking

Think of sentences together that use their spelling words for this week.
(Try to make the sentences funny)
Example:
The tiny bee buzzed so loudly it made him fly backwards.
The giant was looking at the chocolate covered tree.
The girl was jumping so high so almost touched the moon.

Encourage them to think of silly sentences to say out loud.
When you have both thought of some silly sentences encourage them to write out their spelling words.
Help them to sound out their words as they write them.

Grammar
- ❑ Beginning to understand some of the grammar terms used
- ❑ Understanding that verbs are action words
- ❑ confident with writing words
- ❑ Understanding that verbs can be spelt differently if they happen in the past/present.

- ❑ segmenting spoken words into phonemes and representing these by graphemes, spelling many correctly
- ❑ form lower-case letters of the correct size relative to one another

Notes and Assessment of week

26

CHAPTER 5   WEEK 5

Day 1

Warm Up:
Handwriting:
Practice writing high frequency words.

the – was – we – and – of – it – for - they

Model how to write the letters – if you are stuck with this then look on the internet for handwriting practice sheets.

The book I would recommend for handwriting practice at this stage is 'Handwriting Practice Book by Schofield and Sims'.

Introduction: 2 line free verse
Set up a food tasting station: (Be careful of allergies)
Include foods that they like, but also try to think of foods with different textures as well as different taste.
(you could include foods like – lemon, biscuits, banana, ice cream etc)

Main Task:
Explain that you are going to write some poetry – but these poems do not have to have rhyming words.
Share their writing with them encouraging them to write down as much as they feel able to do.
Explain that in the first line they will say what the food is. The second line will tell their reader about the food.
Example:

Creamy ice-cream
Cold and smooth

Slice of lemon
Makes my face go funny

Chocolate biscuit
All crunchy and sticky

Plenary:
Read back their poems together and discussed what they liked about their poems.

Spelling
bank – think – honk – sunk – wink - bunk

Handwriting
- ❑ form lower-case letters of the correct size relative to one another
- ❑ write capital letters and digits of the correct size, orientation and relationship to one another and to lower case letters
- ❑ use spacing between words that reflects the size of the letters.

Poems
- ❑ form lower-case letters of the correct size relative to one another
- ❑ writing about real events
- ❑ writing poetry
- ❑ planning or saying out loud what they are going to write about

Read together a book of their choice.
Help to sound out words that are unfamiliar.

Spelling:
Copy out the spellings list for this week.
Go over the words with them sounding out the phonemes.

WEEK 5

Day 2

Warm Up:
Talk about things they like to do or things they like to eat.
Write down their ideas as they say them.
Explain that you are going to write a poem together about the things they like. Each line of the poem is going to start with the words 'I like ...'

Main Task:
Together look at the list of things they like and choose one.
Write down for them a list of things they like, in the order they want and then cut out each line. (You could type these lines out, print and cut them)

Example:
I like eating cheese on toast
I like playing in the park
I like jumping on my bed
I like cake and custard

Look at the sentence strips together. Talk about putting the sentences into some kind of order. For instance – could they put the sentences about food together in one pile and the things they like to do in another pile?

When they are happy with the order of sentences for their poem, ask them to paste the sentences into their books.

Extra: ICT -
Remind them of how to use the computer to type up their work.
Explain that you are going to use a 'word processor' to publish their poem.
Work together and explain again how to change the font size and colour.

When typing up the title you could introduce how to underline and centre their work.

Once the poem is type up remind them to write at the bottom who the poem is by ...

Read together a book of their choice. Try to find some poetry books at the library.
Help to sound out words that are unfamiliar.

Handwriting Practice
- ❑ form lower-case letters of the correct size relative to one another
- ❑ write capital letters and digits of the correct size, orientation and relationship to one another and to lower case letters
- ❑ use spacing between words that reflects the size of the letters.

Poems
- ❑ form lower-case letters of the correct size relative to one another
- ❑ writing about real events
- ❑ writing poetry
- ❑ planning or saying out loud what they are going to write about
- ❑ encapsulating what they want to say, sentence by sentence
- ❑ learn more functions of a word processing programme
- ❑ Set up and publish work

Handwriting:
Practice letters they are having problems with or work through a handwriting book

28

WEEK 5

Warm Up:
Discuss all the nursery rhymes they know that have numbers and counting in them.
Have a sing-a-long together.
(One, two buckle my shoe, Five Little Current Bun, 1, 2, 3, 4, 5 Once I Saw a Fish Alive, When I was one ...)

Introduction:
Watch 'When I Was One', pirate song on YouTube.

Main Task:
Highlight the number words on the nursery rhyme.
Discuss the rhyming words and highlight the rhyming words in a different colour. **Activity Sheet 26 and 27.**

Read through the nursery rhyme and act out the parts.
(video the reading out and then discuss the performance)

Start a brainstorm of ideas:
Talk about words that rhyme with numbers.
On a large sheet of paper draw out some bubbles with a number in each one. To the outside of the bubble, add any rhyming word you can both think of.

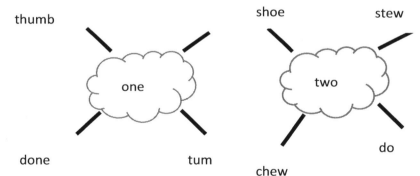

This might not be easy – but it is something to add to over the next few days.

Read together some nursery rhymes.
Pick out any rhyming words you find.
Help to sound out words that are unfamiliar.

Poems
- ☐ form lower-case letters of the correct size relative to one another
- ☐ writing about real events
- ☐ writing poetry
- ☐ planning or saying out loud what they are going to write about
- ☐ encapsulating what they want to say, sentence by sentence
- ☐ brainstorm ideas
- ☐ discover rhyming words
- ☐ learning to appreciate rhymes and poems, and to recite some by heart

Extra
Have a look on the internet together for Nursery Rhymes.
A very good place to start is the BBC.
https://www.bbc.co.uk/programmes/p06kbsbz

Handwriting:
Practice letters they are having problems with or work through a handwriting book

WEEK 5

Day 4

Warm Up:

Introduce the word 'connective'. Talk about it being a type of word that links things together.

Explain that you will be using connectives today to make great sentences.

Write the word **'and'** on one piece of card, and **'because'** on another piece of card.

Take it in turns to say one short sentence.

For example:

"The dog was wagging his tail"

The other person then has to use 'and' or 'because' to expand the sentence.

"<u>because</u> he was happy"

Now it is the next persons turn to start the sentence and the other persons turn to extend it.

To develop the idea of connectives you can add the words **'so' and 'but'**

Introduction:

Watch 'When I Was One', pirate song on YouTube.

Main Task:

Have a look back at the rhyming words on their brainstorm from previous lesson.

Read the nursery rhyme together – change the rhyming words for the ones you have thought of.

For example:

When I was eight,
I was almost late
the day I went to sea

Could become
When I was eight
I shut the gate
The day I went to sea.

Read together some nursery rhymes.

Pick out any rhyming words you find and change them.
Help to sound out words that are unfamiliar.

Connectives:

Connectives are words that link ideas together in separate sentences or paragraphs.

In the primary curriculum children are encouraged to talk about connectives using grammatical terms (conjunction, proposition and adverb). Connectives is an umbrella term to describe all of these.

We use <u>**co-ordinating conjunctions**</u> to join two parts of a sentence that are of equal weight or importance.

A <u>**subordinating conjunction**</u> introduces a **subordinate clause** (a clause that does not make sense on its own).

Here are some examples of connectives:

Adding – and, moreover, also, as well as, furthermore.

Time – next, then, finally, meanwhile, eventually

Cause/Effect: because, therefore, so, as a result of

Contrasting: however, alternatively, although, except, unless

Handwriting:

Write out connectives for handwriting practice
and, because, so, but

Spelling:

Remind them of the spelling words for this week.

WEEK 5

Day 5

Introduction: ICT

More practice using a word processor on the computer.
Let them watch while you're opening the word program – explain what you are doing as you do it.

Main Task:

Type out the first part of a short sentence for them.
For example:
The lion stared at the mouse
Ask them to change the colour of the text and add a connective word – then you finish off the sentence with their ideas.
The lion stared at the mouse ***because*** he was hungry.

To extend this ask them to type more of the sentence themselves.

Spelling

Testing of the spelling words for this week.

ba**nk** – thi**nk** – ho**nk** – su**nk** – wi**nk** – bunk

Think of sentences together that use their spelling words for this week.
(Try to make the sentences funny)

Encourage them to think of silly sentences to say out loud.
When you have both thought of some silly sentences encourage them to write out their spelling words.
Help them to sound out their words as they write them.

Grammar

- ❑ Using connectives
- ❑ subordination (using when, if, that, or because) and co-ordination (using or, and, or but)
- ❑ How words can combine to make sentences Joining words and joining clauses using 'and'
- ❑ Extend to using other connectives

- ❑ segmenting spoken words into phonemes and representing these by graphemes, spelling many correctly
- ❑ form lower-case letters of the correct size relative to one another

Read together a book of their choice. **Help to sound out words that are unfamiliar.**

Notes and Assessment of week

1

Day 1

Warm Up:
Read a story to them without them looking at the book.
Explain before you start reading that you want them to clap every time a full stop, question mark or explanation mark is used in the book.
When they have clapped, let them check the text with you to see if they were correct.

Introduction:
Discuss the words that rhymed in the nursery rhyme 'When I was one', and all the other rhyming words you found together.

Main Task:
Spot the word that does not rhyme in the group.
Activity Sheet 28.
Read the words together and ask them to listen for the odd one out.
Put a circle around the word.

Choose one of the words and ask them to write it in a bubble (the same way that the bubbles were made for 'When I was one'.
Ask them to write down as many words they can think of that rhyme. (help with spellings and ideas).

With there chosen word ask them to write a sentence with that word at the end.
I can see a **dog**
Now ask them to choose a rhyming word and write another sentence –

I can see a **dog**

Going for a **jog**

Spelling
Read these words together. **chip - chick - catch – fetch - kitchen - notch - rich - much - such – hutch**

Write out the words in bright colours on small pieces of card.
Turn the cards face down. Take turns to pick up a card and read it.
Demonstrate how to sound out the phonemes.

Grammar
- ❏ Developing an understanding of what a sentence is.
- ❏ learning how to use both familiar and new punctuation correctly, including full stops, capital letters, exclamation marks, question marks

Poems
- ❏ form lower-case letters of the correct size relative to one another
- ❏ writing about real events
- ❏ writing poetry
- ❏ planning or saying out loud what they are going to write about
- ❏ encapsulating what they want to say, sentence by sentence
- ❏ brainstorm ideas
- ❏ discover rhyming words
- ❏ learning to appreciate rhymes and poems, and to recite some by heart

Spelling rules for this week's words.

The sound /ch/ spelt 'ch'
The sound /ch/ spelt –'tch'

WEEK 6

Day 2

Warm Up:

Action Verb Game. **Activity Sheet 29**

Close your eyes and point to one of the action verbs.

Do the action as quick as you can. Your partners will guess what the verb is as quickly as they can.

Then it is the next persons go.

Who can do the best actions?

Introduction:

Explain that you will be writing a poem called 'My Family'. You can introduce the word **ACROSTIC** and tell them that an acrostic poem spells out a word – but it does not need to rhyme.

Together think of some words that might describe your family and write them down for them.

Main Task:

Write down MY FAMILY down the side of the page. Explain that each line is going to start with that letter.

For example:

M um helps me.

Y ellow is dad's favourite colour.

F ood is cooked in the kitchen.

A lice is my auntie.

M

I

L

Y

Play a game of writing one line each. Think of the sentences together.

Explain that the poem can be made up and can be funny, it does not have to be true.

Encourage sentence writing and use of full stops.

Grammar

❑ Beginning to understand some of the grammar terms used

❑ Understanding that verbs are action words

❑ confident with writing words

❑ Understanding that verbs can be spelt differently if they happen in the

Poems

❑ form lower-case letters of the correct size relative to one another

❑ Using full stops correctly

❑ Leaving spaces between words

❑ writing about real or imagined events

❑ writing poetry

❑ encapsulating what they want to say, sentence by sentence

❑ brainstorm ideas

❑ learning to appreciate rhymes and poems, and to recite some by heart

Read together a book of their choice. Try to find some poetry books at the library.

Help to sound out words that are unfamiliar.

Extra: ICT

Together type up the acrostic poem to be printed out.

Encourage them to draw a frame around the poem using small images

WEEK 6

Day 3/4

Introduction: Grammar

Recap on what a noun is.

Talk about when you looked at days of the week and how the days of the week always start with a capital letter.

Remind them that the days of the week are proper nouns, so they always start with a capital letter.

Ask them if they think the months of the year are proper nouns.

Main Task:

Look at a calendar that shows a month on the page if you have one (you can easily find one online if you do not have one you can use).

Read the months together. Notice how the start with a capital letter.

Sing the song together about the months of the year. (if you cannot remember the song you will find examples on You Tube – just type in 'months of the year song' and you will find a lot of examples.

Main Task:

Ask them to write out the months of the year in order to help them remember them. You will need to help them with the spellings of the words.

Encourage the to write out the words in different colours.

Read together a book of their choice. Try to find some poetry books at the library.

Help to sound out words that are unfamiliar.

Recap:

Have a look at the noun, adjective and verb work covered over the last six weeks.

Ask them if they can give you examples of what the words mean.

Can they tell you what a character is?

Do they remember what protagonist means?

Can they explain, or give an example, of a setting?

Have a look back at the sentences and poems they have written.

What do they think about their work?

Tell them you are really proud of all the work they have done.

Capital Letters and Full Stops

- ❑ Separation of words with spaces Introduction to capital letters, full stops, question marks and exclamation marks to demarcate sentences Capital letters for names and for the personal pronoun I
- ❑ form lower-case letters of the correct size relative to one another
- ❑ use spacing between words that reflects the size of the letters

- ❑ segmenting spoken words into phonemes and representing these by graphemes, spelling many correctly
- ❑ form lower-case letters of the correct size relative to one another

WEEK 6

<u>Last task of the unit is the Spelling Test</u>
Testing of the spelling words for this week.

chip - chick - catch – fetch - kitchen - notch - rich - much - such – hutch

Ask them to sound out the words and try to write them correctly.

Notes and Assessment of unit

Sheet 1

Adjectives you might use to describe a setting

bright	big
drab	colossal
elegant	enormous
filthy	gigantic
grotesque	great
long	huge
magnificent	large
sparkling	little
spotless	long
strange	massive
dark	mighty
smelly	mini
bright	small

23.

36

Can you help me fill in the missing words? They seemed to have dropped to the bottom of the

The wolf made a big .... and a

.... and he blew the house

down.

Don't jump .... the .... it is

too high.

cliff   huff   off   puff

Features of a Recount

The most important things to remember is how to set the scene.

Think about

who, what, where, when and how

This recount is going to be about **you** so that is who.

Now think about when it happened.

Now all you have to think about is where and what happened, and maybe why.

This is going to be about something that happened in the past. It might have happened yesterday, or last week, or even a long time ago. This is what is called 'past tense'.

My Recount of My Day Out

First	Then

After that	Finally

Capital Letters and Full Stops

Oh No! A thief has stolen all the capital letters and full stops.
Can you find where the capital letters and the full stops should be?

jack went up the beanstalk

on monday the cats lost their mittens

the cat went to london to visit the queen

goldilocks ate all the porridge in the small bowl

jack and jill went up the hill

miss muffet sat on a tuffet eating her curds and whey

Can you draw the vegetables from the story?	

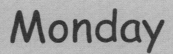

Monday

On Monday

Tuesday

Wednesday

Thursday

Friday

Saturday

Sunday

My Book Review

I liked _____

The main character is _____

The setting is _____

Name that Noun

PHASE 3 PHONICS

BY THE TIME THEY REACH PHASE 3, CHILDREN WILL ALREADY BE ABLE TO BLEND AND SEGMENT WORDS CONTAINING THE 19 LETTERS TAUGHT IN PHASE 2. IN THIS PHASE, TWENTY-FIVE NEW GRAPHEMES ARE INTRODUCED (ONE AT A TIME).

SET 6: j, v, w, x

SET 7: y, z, zz, qu

CONSONANT DIGRAPHS: ch, sh, th, ng

VOWEL DIGRAPHS: ai, ee, igh, oa, oo, ar, or, ur, ow, oi, ear, air, ure, er

DURING PHASE 3, LEARN THE LETTER NAMES USING AN ALPHABET SONG, BUT CONTINUE TO USE THE SOUNDS WHEN DECODING WORDS.

TRICKY WORDS

DURING PHASE 3, THE FOLLOWING TRICKY WORDS (WHICH CAN'T YET BE DECODED) ARE INTRODUCED:

he   she   we   me   be   was   you   they

all   are   my   her

FOR A LIST OF PHASE 3 PHONICS GO TO http://www.letters-and-sounds.com/

1

Can you sound out these words?

jog	vet	wax	zip
win	buzz	jazz	sing
hang	shop	gift	soft

READ THESE WORDS AND DRAW A PICTURE

fish	ring	king
web	van	ship

Read this story together, then see if you can answer the questions.

Bobby got out of bed feeling very happy. He was going to the seaside with Mum, Dad and sister Jenny.

He washed and brushed his teeth. Then he put on his blue shorts and bright yellow tea-shirt. He loved his yellow tea-shirt because it had a picture of a dragon on it.

Dad was busy in the kitchen making sandwiches.

Mum helped him put on his coat. "It might get cold later," she said.

Bobby and Jenny raced to the car and jumped in the back seats.

Mum and Dad followed. When they were all settled in the car with seatbelts on, they set off on their fantastic adventure.

Where was Bobby going?

Bobby was going to the ....

What did bobby love?

Bobby loved his ....

Bobby's sisters name is ....

Dad was busy making .... in the kitchen.

Mum said, 'It might get .... later.

3

CUT OUT THESE WORDS AND ARRANGE THEM INTO SENTENCES

WHAT STORY DO YOU THINK IT'S GOING TO BE?

man	Stop	catch	said	Gingerbread
the	Run	you	can't	little
me	said	as	I'm	The
Gingerbread	you	the	man	He
run	the	ran	lady	hill
fast	old	can	down	as
.	.	!	.	.

THE GINGERBREAD MAN

Once upon a time, there was a little old woman and a little old man.
They both lived in a little cottage by a river.
The little old man said, "I'm just going to work in the garden dear
wife."
The little old lady smiled and said, "Then I will make you a lovely
gingerbread biscuit to eat."

She made a big batch of gingerbread dough, then rolled it flat.
Then she thought that her husband might like his gingerbread cut
into the shape of a man. So, she cut the shape of a gingerbread
man out of the dough.
She gave him raisins for eyes, a drop of icing for a mouth, and
chocolate chips for buttons. Then she put the gingerbread man in
the oven to bake.

When the gingerbread man was done, the little old woman opened
the oven door, but before she could take him out, the gingerbread
man jumped up and ran through the kitchen and out of the
cottage shouting, "You're not going to eat me!"

The little old woman ran after the gingerbread man . "Stop," she
shouted.
But the gingerbread man ran even faster, chanting, "<u>Run, run as
fast as you can. You can't catch me, I'm the gingerbread
man.</u>"

The gingerbread man ran into the garden and passed the little old man.

"Stop," the little old man called out, "I want to eat you."

But the gingerbread man ran even faster, chanting, "I've run away from a little old woman, and I can run away from you, I can, I can. <u>Run, run as fast as you can. You can't catch me, I'm the gingerbread man."</u>

The little old man chased the gingerbread man, followed by the little old woman. But the gingerbread man ran too fast for them. The gingerbread man ran through the garden and passed a pig.

"Stop," the pig snorted, "I want to eat you."

But the gingerbread man ran even faster, chanting, "I've run from a little old woman and a little old man, and I can run away from you, I can, I can. <u>Run, run as fast as you can. You can't catch me, I'm the gingerbread man."</u>

The pig chased the gingerbread man, followed by the little old woman and the little old man. But the gingerbread man ran too fast for them.

The gingerbread man passed a cow int the field. "Stop," the cow mooed, "I want to eat you."

But the gingerbread man ran even faster, chanting, "I've run from a little old woman and a little old man and a pig, and I can run away from you, I can, I can. <u>Run, run as fast as you can. You can't catch me, I'm the gingerbread man.</u>"

The cow chased the gingerbread man, followed by the pig and the little old woman and the little old man. But the gingerbread man ran too fast for them.

The gingerbread man passed a horse in the field. "Stop," the horse neighed, "I want to eat you."

But the gingerbread man ran even faster, chanting, "I've run from a little old woman and a little old man and a pig and a cow, and I can run away from you, I can, I can. <u>Run, run as fast as you can. You can't catch me, I'm the gingerbread man</u>."

The horse chased the gingerbread man, followed by the cow, the pig, and the little old woman and the little old man. But the gingerbread man ran too fast for them.

He was very pleased with himself and feeling very clever. But then he reached a wide river. Now, there was a problem, because the gingerbread man didn't know how to swim.

He sat on a rock and thought for a while.

There was a sly fox watching him. He was a very hungry fox.

"Hello little gingerbread man. Are you in trouble?" he said sweetly.

"You can't eat me. I've run away from a horse, a cow, a pig, a little old woman and a little old man. I can run away from you," said the gingerbread man.

The sly fox smiled and said "I just want to help you. I can get you across the river."
"Thank you so much," said the gingerbread man.

"Jump on my tail, and I'll take you across the river!"

The gingerbread man thought to himself, "I'll be safe on his tail."
So, he jumped on the fox's tail and they started across the river.

Halfway across the river, the fox barked, "You're too heavy for my tail, jump on my back."
So, the gingerbread man jumped on the fox's back.

Soon, the fox said, you're too heavy for my back, jump onto my nose."
So, the gingerbread man jumped on the fox's nose.

But as soon as they reached the riverbank, the fox flipped the gingerbread man into the air, snapped his mouth shut, and ate the gingerbread man ALL IN ONE BIG GULP.

And that was the end of the gingerbread man.

GINGERBREAD MAN RECIPE

You will need:

75g......... unsalted butter (softened)
150g....... soft light brown sugar
350g....... plain flour
1 tsp....... bicarbonate of soda
2 tsp......ground ginger
4 tbsp...golden syrup or honey
1............ egg (beaten)
2 tbsp.. freshly squeezed orange juice
Currents, raisins or sweets to decorate.

1   Cream the butter and the sugar.

2   Add the flour, bicarbonate of soda and ginger and stir well.

3   Measure the golden syrup or honey into a small microwaveable bowl and warm in the microwave until runny. Mix with the beaten egg, then add to the flour mixture and mix well.

4   Mix in the orange juice a little at a time until a dough forms. Shape it into a flat disc, wrap tightly in cling film and chill for 30 minutes

5   Preheat the oven to 180°C/Mark 4 and line two baking trays with non-stick baking paper

6   Roll out the dough on a lightly floured work surface and shape out gingerbread men. Place them on the prepared trays, spacing them at least 3cm apart, and chill for at least another 15 minutes.

7   Bake for about 15 minutes, or until the biscuits are dry on top and slightly darker than when they went in the oven. Allow to cool on their trays for about 10 minutes, then use a palette knife to transfer them carefully to a wire rack. They will harden as they cool.

8   Decorate the gingerbread men with currants, raisins or sweets when cold using a tiny bit of melted chocolate or icing to stick them on.

When I was one,
I sucked my thumb,
the day I went to sea.
I climbed aboard a pirate ship - and the captain said to me:
we're going this way, that way, - forwards backwards, over the Irish sea.
A bottle of rum to fill my tum, a pirates' life for me'.

When I was two,
I buckled my shoe,
the day I went to sea.
I climbed aboard a pirate ship - and the captain said to me:
we're going this way, that way, forwards backwards, over the Irish sea.
A bottle of rum to fill my tum, a pirate's life for me'.

When I was three,
I grazed my knee,
the day I went to sea.
I climbed aboard a pirate ship - and the captain said to me:
we're going this way, that way, forwards backwards, over the Irish sea.
A bottle of rum to fill my tum, a pirate's life for me'.

When I was four,
I swam ashore,
the day I went to sea.
I climbed aboard a pirate ship - and the captain said to me:
we're going this way, that way, forwards backwards, over the Irish sea.
A bottle of rum to fill my tum, a pirate's life for me'.

When I was five,
I learned to dive,
the day I went to sea.
I climbed aboard a pirate ship - and the captain said to me:
we're going this way, that way, forwards backwards, over the Irish sea.
A bottle of rum to fill my tum, a pirate's life for me'.

When I was six,
I gathered sticks,
the day I went to sea.
I climbed aboard a pirate ship - and the captain said to me:
'we're going this way, that way, forwards backwards, over the Irish sea.
A bottle of rum to fill my tum
a pirate's life for me'.

When I was seven,
I went to Devon,
the day I went to sea.
I climbed aboard a pirate ship - and the captain said to me:
'we're going this way, that way, forwards backwards, over the Irish sea.
A bottle of rum to fill my tum
a pirate's life for me'.

When I was eight,
I was almost late
the day I went to sea.
I climbed aboard a pirate ship - and the captain said to me:
'we're going this way, that way, forwards backwards, over the Irish sea.
A bottle of rum to fill my tum
a pirate's life for me'.

When I was nine,
I was feeling fine,
the day I went to sea.
I climbed aboard a pirate ship - and the captain said to me:
'we're going this way, that way, forwards backwards, over the Irish sea.
A bottle of rum to fill my tum
a pirate's life for me'.

When I was ten,
I started again,
the day I went to sea.
I climbed aboard a pirate ship - and the captain said to me:
'we're going this way, that way, forwards backwards, over the Irish sea.
A bottle of rum to fill my tum
a pirate's life for me'.

ODD ONE OUT

cat	mat	dog	hat
hen	pen	den	slug
dog	frog	log	sat
box	bed	fox	ox
red	head	frog	ted
cake	cat	rake	Jake

ACTION VERB GAME

jump	wave	rake	drive
eat	shave	zip	march
write	hug	chase	wash
sleep	skip	skate	sing
tap	paste	paddle	walk
kick	wash	clap	run
hop	jog	drink	dance
talk	sweep	brush	mix
tickle	twirl	sit	twist

ABOUT THE AUTHOR

Hi, dear readers. My name is Denise. I am a wife – mother – grandmother and retired teacher.
I loved teaching, and I did it for over twenty years. I also spent three years child-minding. So, you could say I've worked with children from 0 to 12 for most of my life.
I had to give up teaching because of family circumstances. Do I miss it? Yes, I do.
The trouble is, once teaching is in your blood there is not much you can do about it.
I started the website at that time and that allowed me to share some of my passion with others.
Then it was decided that I should home-school my grandson. I jumped at the chance and was very happy to do so. So, I'm back teaching. But now I can teach the way I know works best. And that is through having as much fun as possible.
Then I started a Facebook page and that really started to develop. It was great chatting with adults and sharing ideas.
And for a while, all of that was enough. But I saw that a lot of people that are homeschooling lacked in confidence and needed just a little help along the way. Our Facebook group grew and grew with everybody helping each other and giving each other ideas.
I published two Science topic books, with more to follow. The first one is called 'Wonderful Humans' and the second one is 'Wonderful Forces and Electricity'. These are dip in and out of books and are not intended to be structured in any way.

Now I want to help more people by sharing some ideas for structured Literacy Lessons.
Some lessons, like Literacy, sometimes need a more structured approach. But it is difficult to know where to start.

The Facebook page is Learn at home.
The website is www.whyplay.co
You will find extra resources to go with this book on the website under 'extra for books'

Printed in Great
Britain
by Amazon